HAL•LEONARD

T-BONE WALKER

CONTENTS

Cover Photo by Jan Persson/Redferns

ISBN 978-1-4768-1392-9

HAL•LEONARD®
CORPORATION
7777 W. BLUEMOUND RD. P.O. BOX 13819 MILWAUKEE, WI 53213

Visit Hal Leonard Online at
www.halleonard.com

Glamour Girl

Words and Music by Aaron "T-Bone" Walker

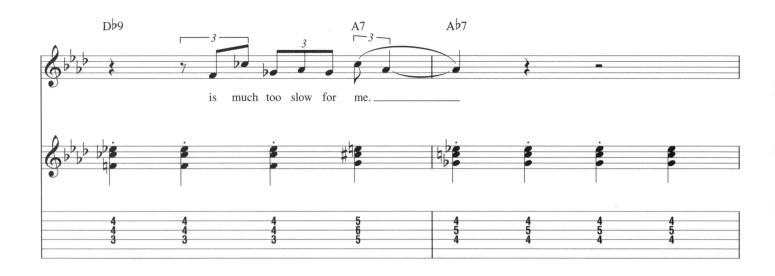

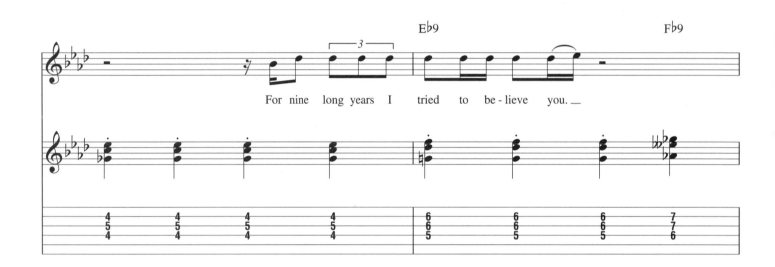

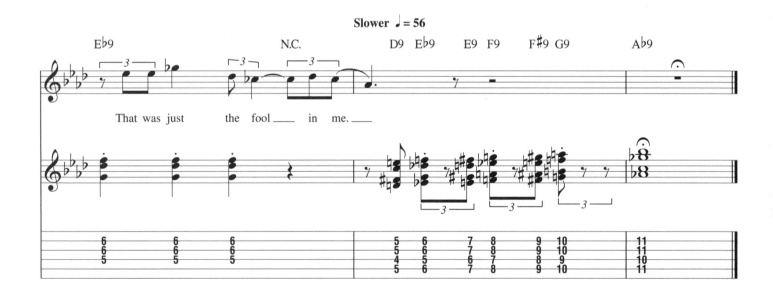

Additional Lyrics

3. Twelve o'clock is rising hour.
   You think that's a crime.
   You better getcha another place for Charlie,
   'Cause I'm through feedin' ya mine.

I Got a Break Baby

Words and Music by Aaron "T-Bone" Walker

*Chord symbols reflect implied harmony.

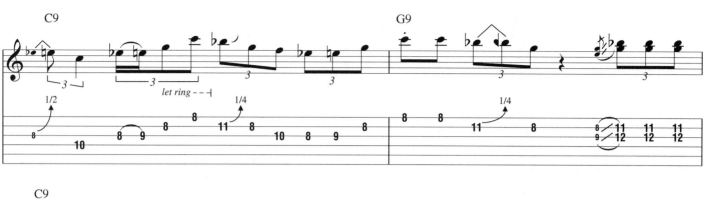

*Played as even eighth notes.

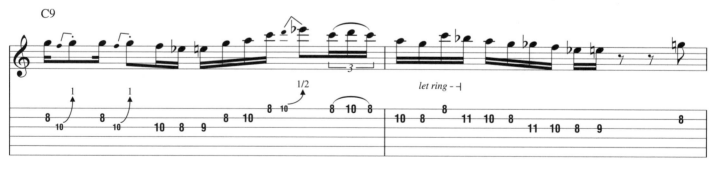

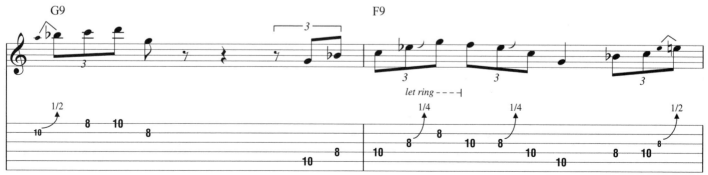

*Sung as even eighth notes.

Mean Old World

Words and Music by Aaron "T-Bone" Walker and Marl Young

Intro
Moderately slow ♩ = 90

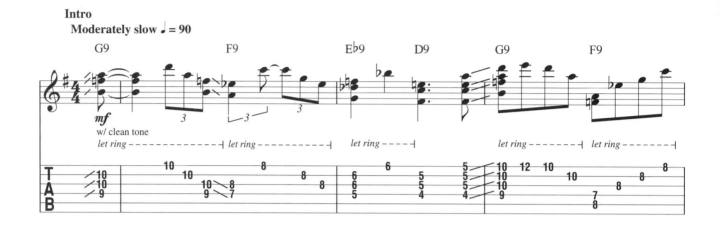

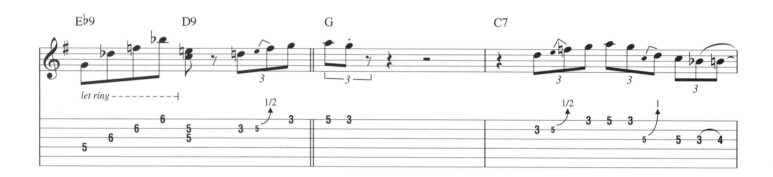

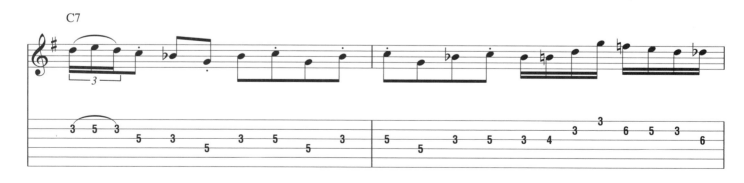

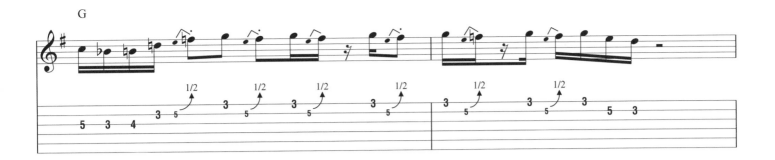

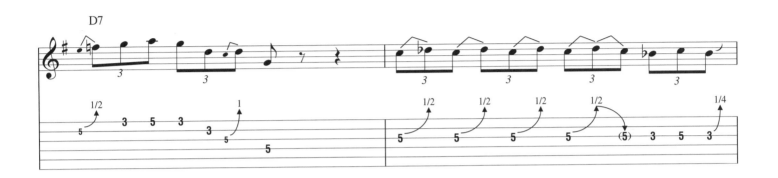

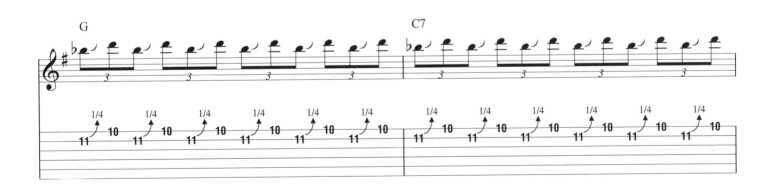

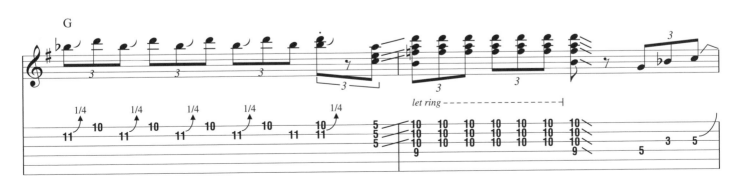

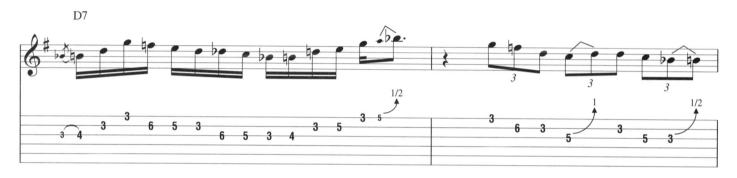

1. This is

Verse

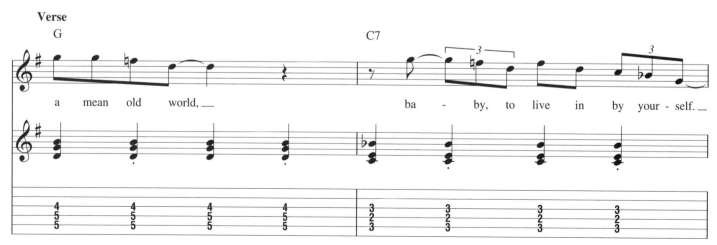

a   mean old   world, __   ba - by, to   live   in   by   your - self. __

Papa Ain't Salty

Words and Music by T-Bone Walker and Grover McDaniel

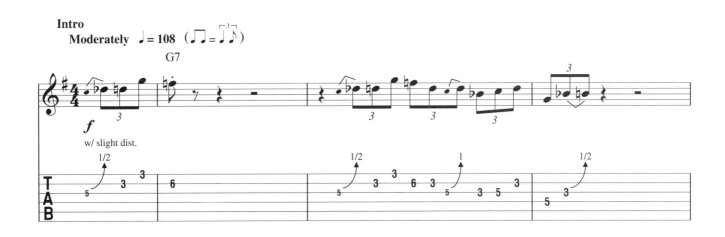

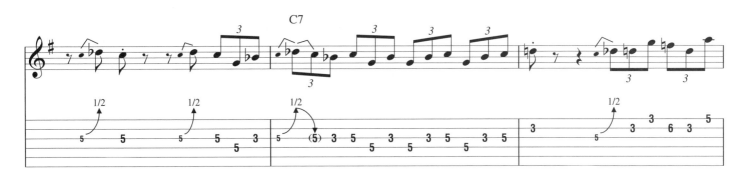

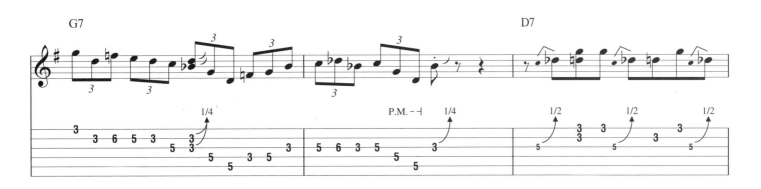

Verse

_____ lit - tle girl, _____ your pap' ain't salt - y no more. _

Come _ home _____ lit - tle girl, _____ your pap' ain't salt - y no more. _

_____ I _____ need _____ your _ love _____

and I _____ swear I _____ miss you so. _____ 2. I know I _____

Verse

_____ was wrong, _____ and I _____ know I've _ caused you pains. _

I know I _____ was wrong, _____ and I _____ know I've _ caused you pains. _

_____ I'm _ sor - ry pret - ty ba - by, _

I won't do that a - gain._____

Guitar Solo

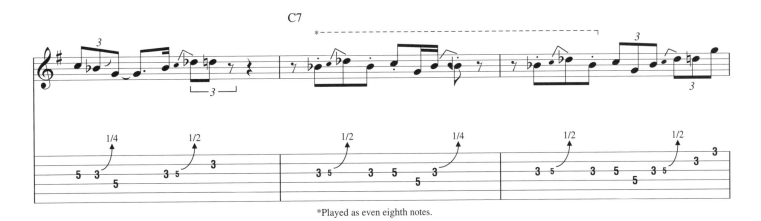

*Played as even eighth notes.

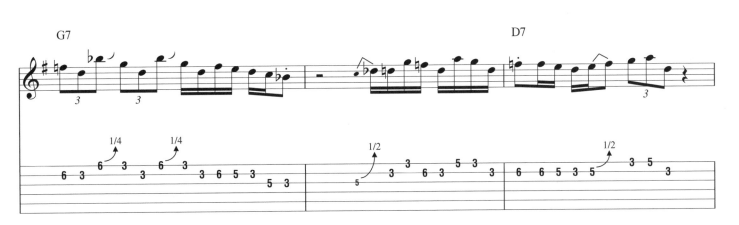

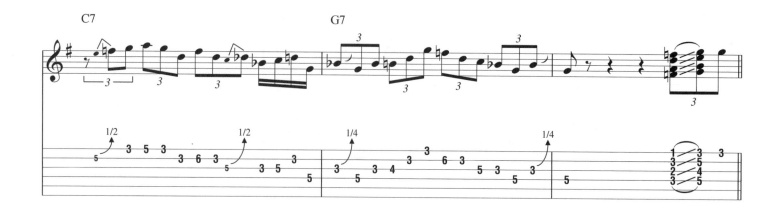

Interlude

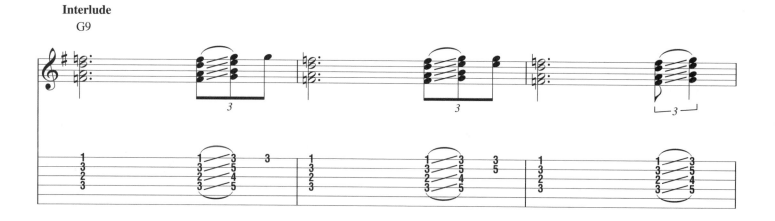

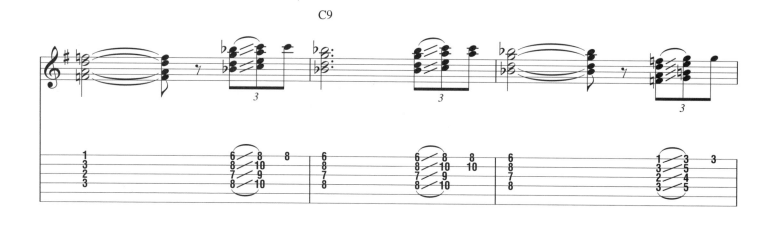

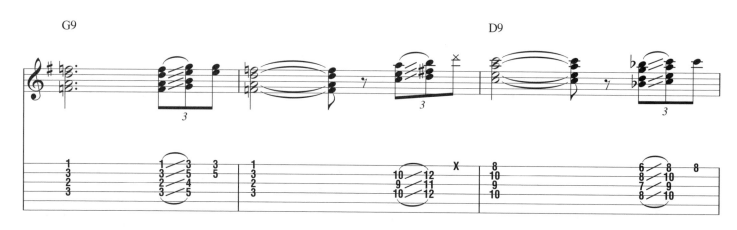

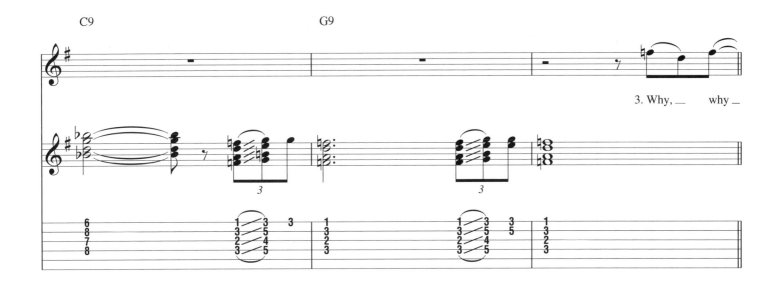

Verse
Gtr. tacet

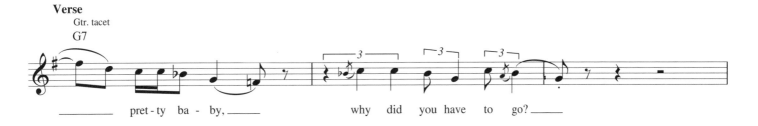

pret - ty ba - by, ____ why did you have to go? ____

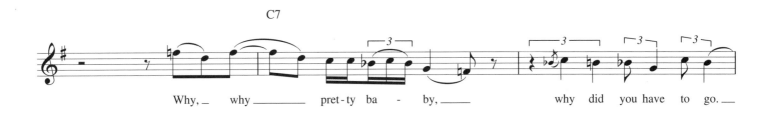

Why, ___ why ____ pret-ty ba - by, _____ why did you have to go. ____

Please ___ come back ____ home ___ pret - ty ma - ma, ____

pap' ain't salt - y no more. ____

(They Call It) Stormy Monday
(Stormy Monday Blues)

Words and Music by Aaron "T-Bone" Walker

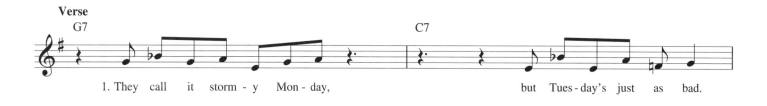

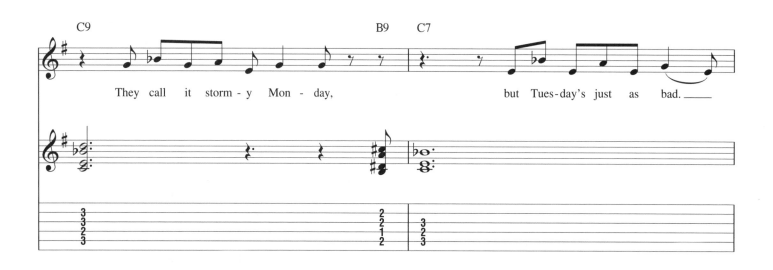

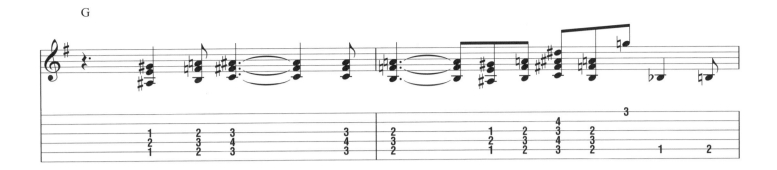

Wednes - day's worse, __ and __ Thurs - day's al - so sad. __

__ 2. Yes, _____

Verse

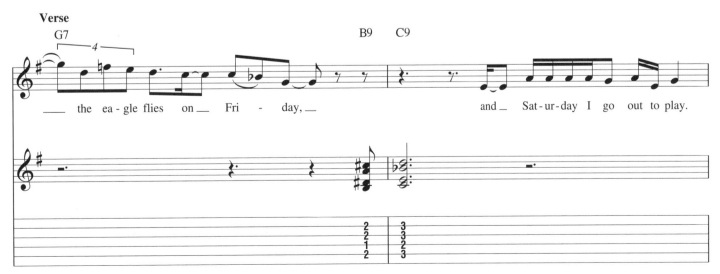

__ the ea - gle flies on __ Fri - day, __ and __ Sat - ur-day I go out to play.

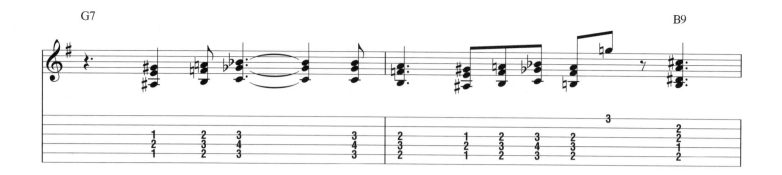

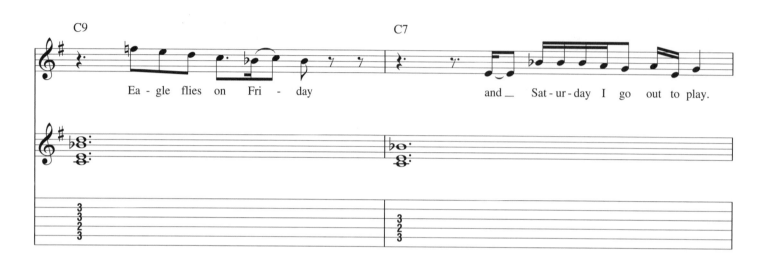

Ea - gle flies on Fri - day   and __ Sat - ur - day I go out to play.

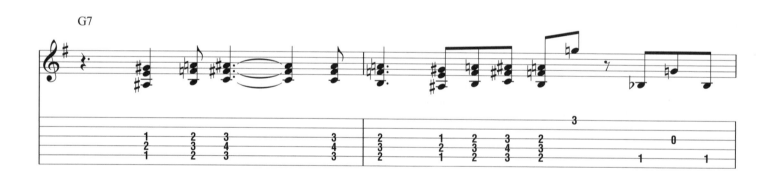

Sun-day I go to church,   then I __ kneel __ down and

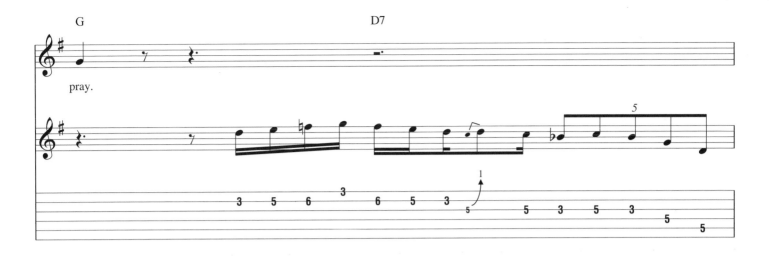

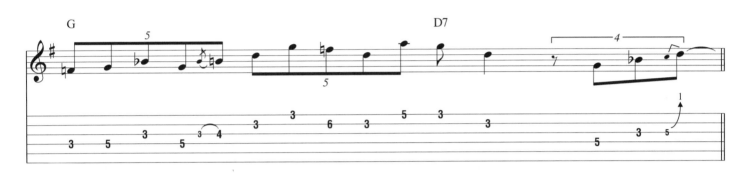

Guitar Solo

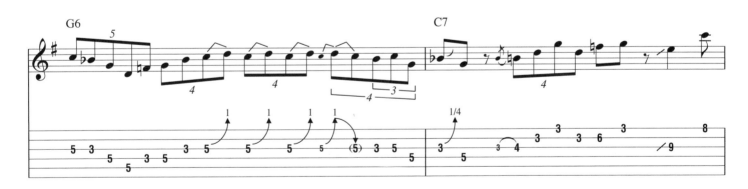

Verse

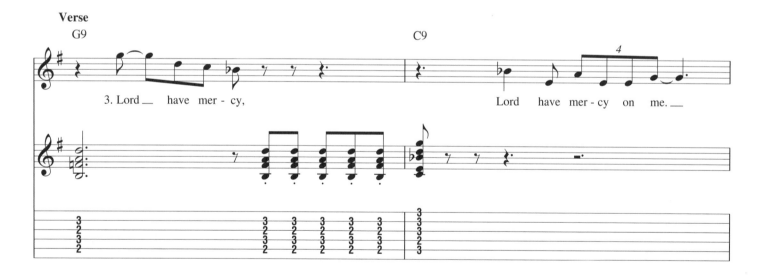

3. Lord __ have mer - cy,   Lord   have mer - cy   on   me. __

Strollin' with Bones

Words and Music by T-Bone Walker, Vida Lee Walker and Edward Davis, Jr.

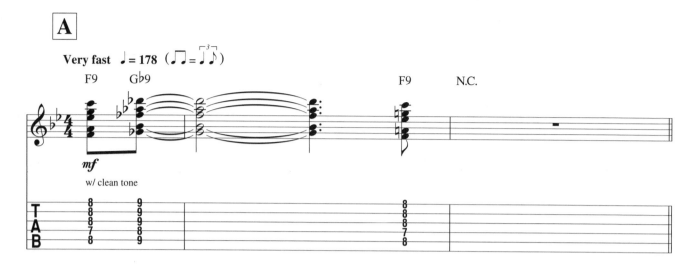

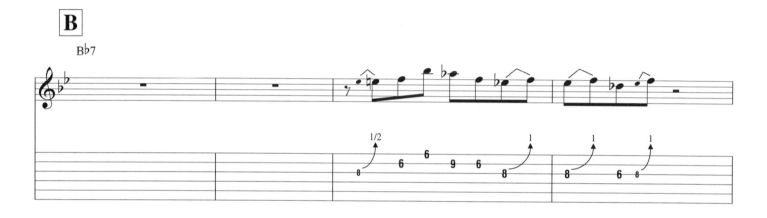

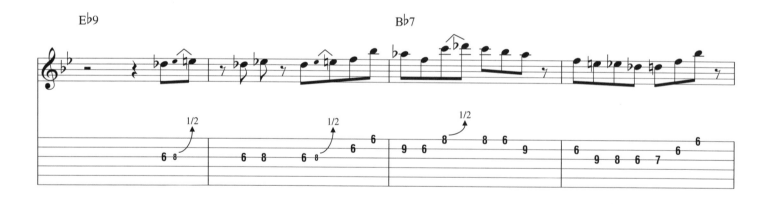

*Played as even eighth notes.

*Played as even eighth notes.

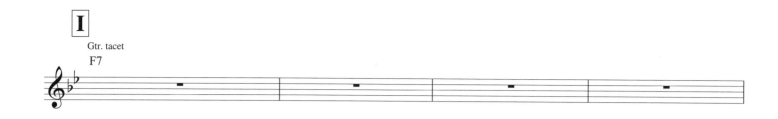

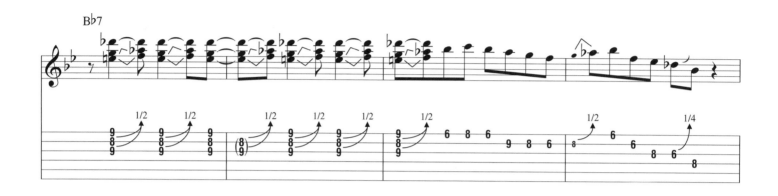

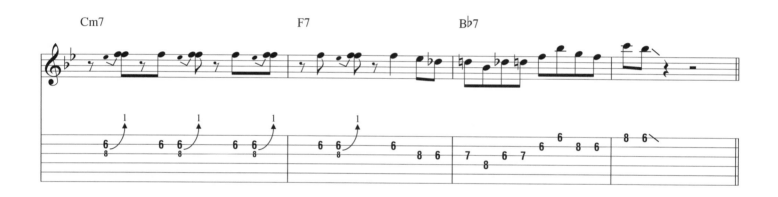

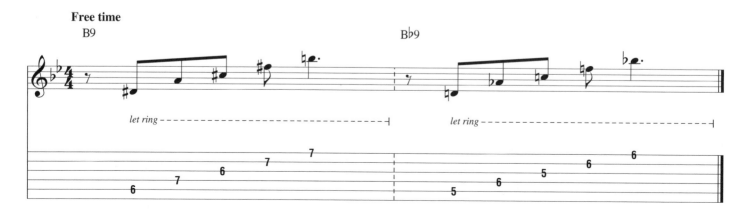

T-Bone Jumps Again

Words and Music by Aaron "T-Bone" Walker

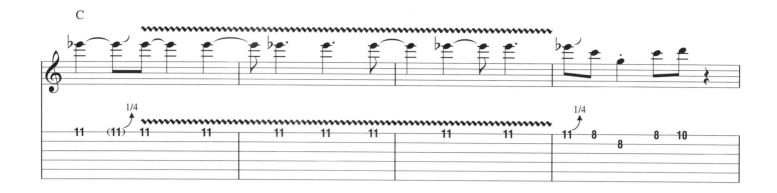

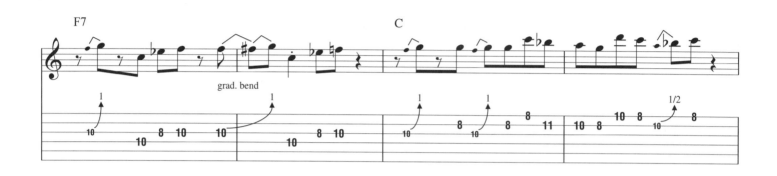

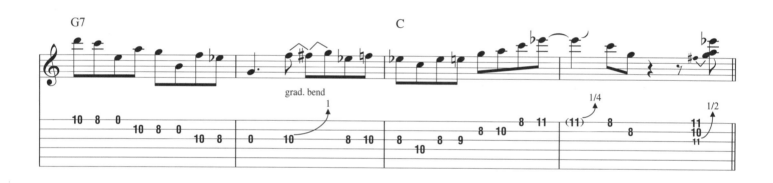

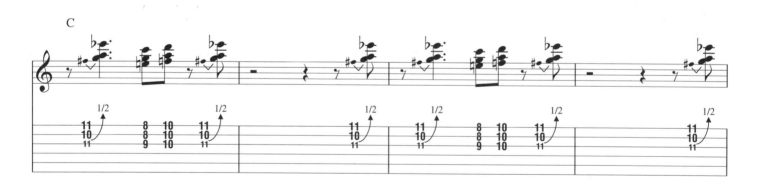

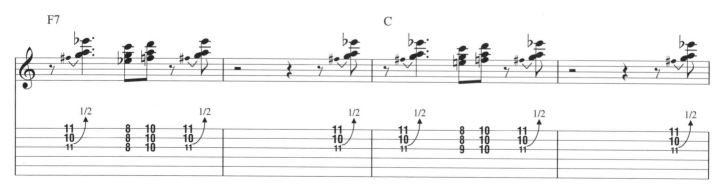

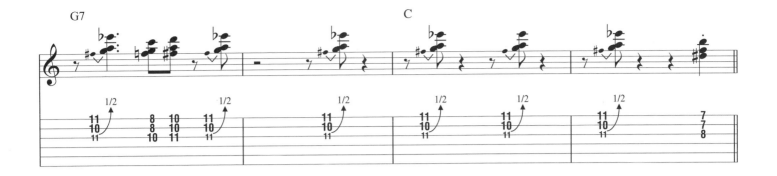

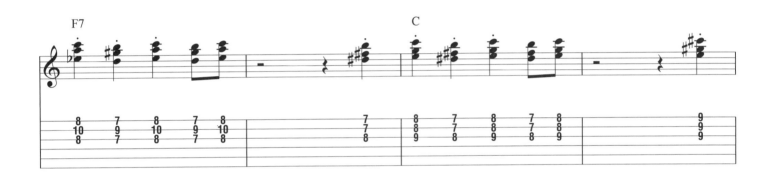

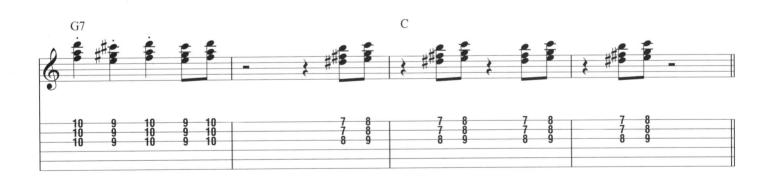

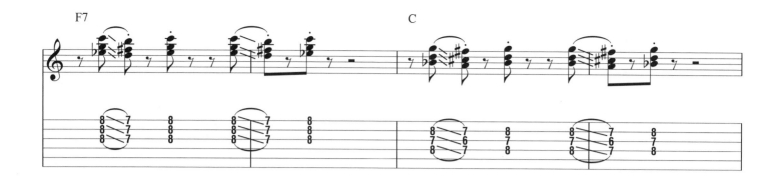

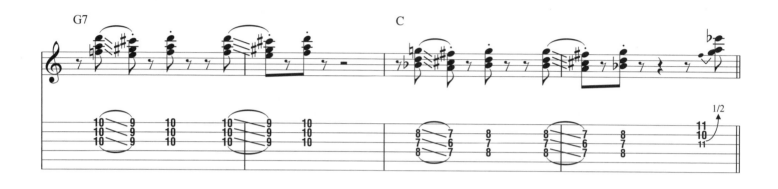

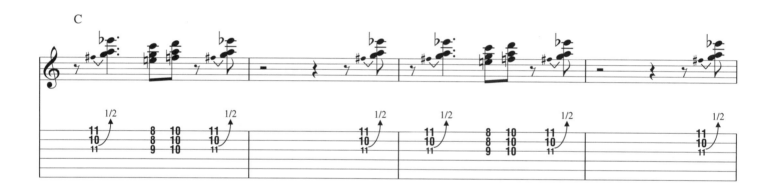

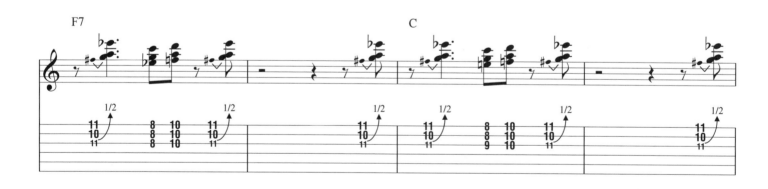

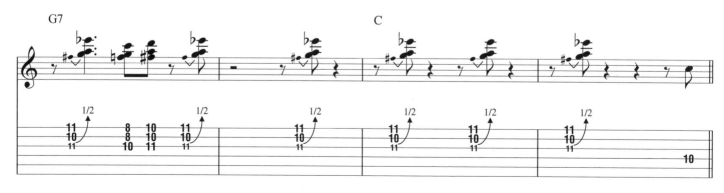

You Don't Love Me

Words and Music by Aaron "T-Bone" Walker and Marl Young

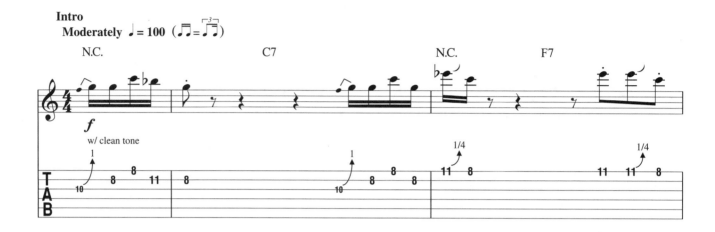

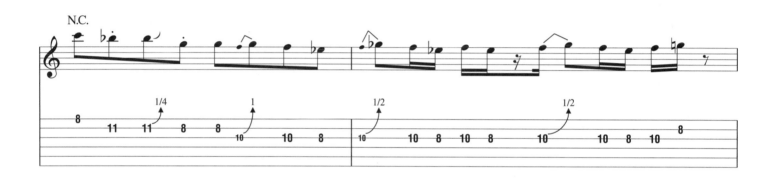

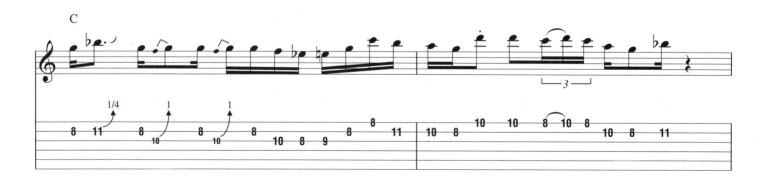

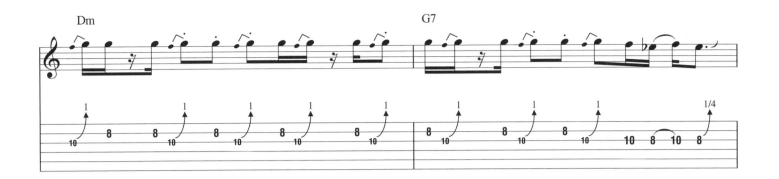

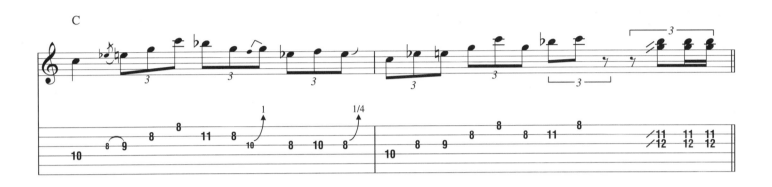

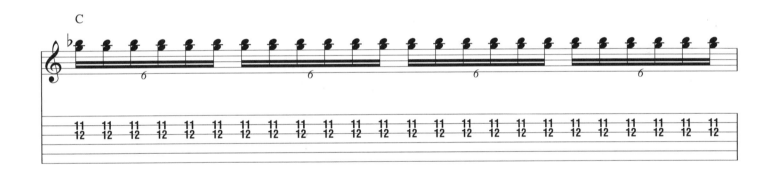

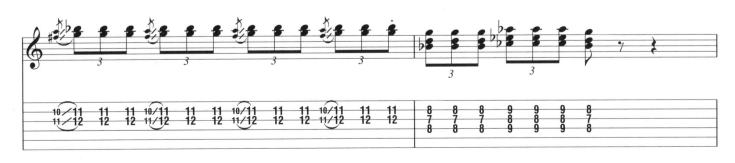

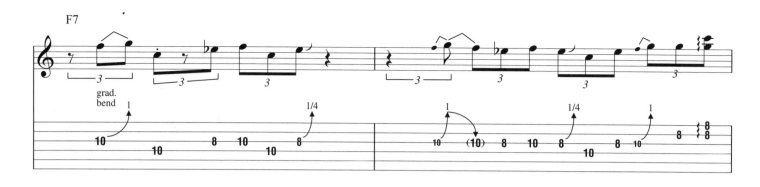

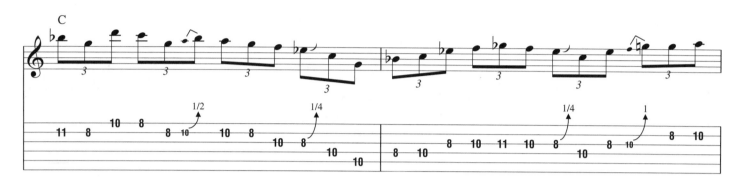

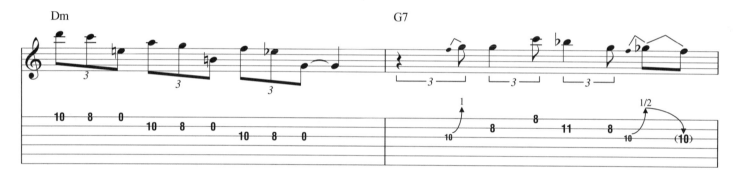

Verse

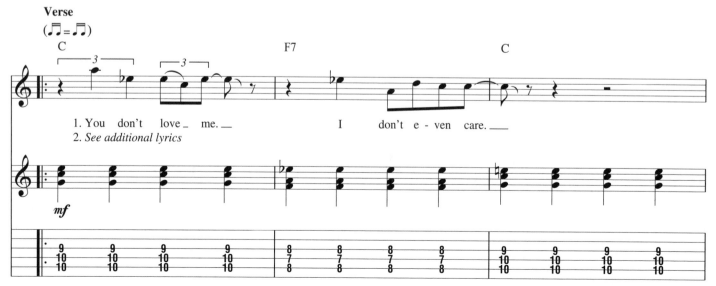

1. You don't love me. I don't e-ven care.

2. *See additional lyrics*

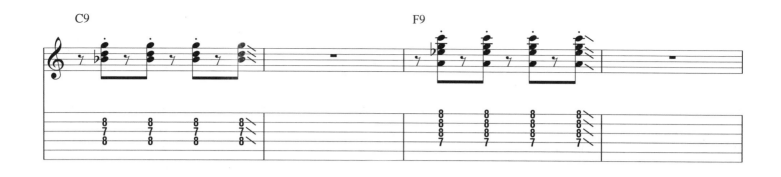

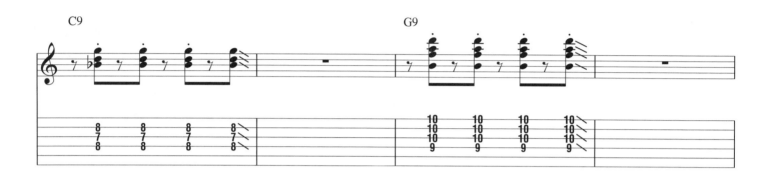

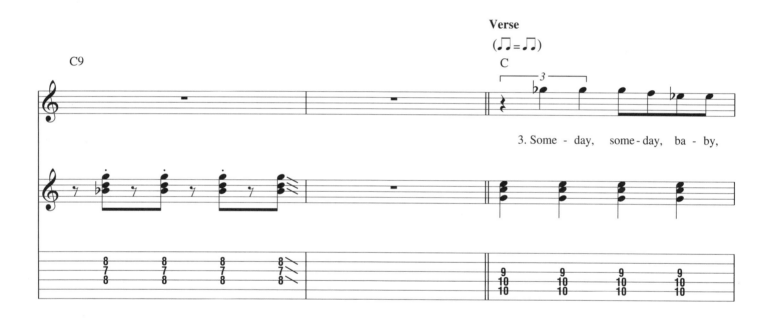

3. Some - day,   some - day, ba - by,

mom - ma, when you change your way,

some - day, some-day, ba - by, mom-ma, when you change your way,____

then things will be dif - f'rent, dar - lin';_____

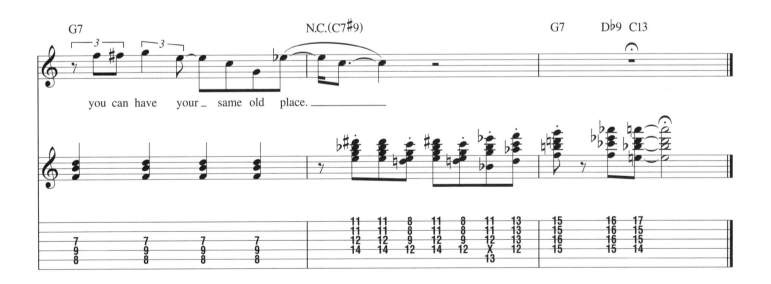

you can have your_ same old place._____

Additional Lyrics

2. Bye, bye, baby.
   Momma, if you call I'm gone.
   Bye, bye, baby.
   Momma, if you call I'm gone.
   I've got a brand new woman, darlin',
   To move in your happy home.

HAL•LEONARD GUITAR PLAY•ALONG®

This series will help you play your favorite songs quickly and easily. Just follow the tab and listen to the CD to the hear how the guitar should sound, and then play along using the separate backing tracks. Mac or PC users can also slow down the tempo without changing pitch by using the CD in their computer. The melody and lyrics are included in the book so that you can sing or simply follow along.

INCLUDES TAB

VOL. 1 – ROCK	00699570 / $16.99	
VOL. 2 – ACOUSTIC	00699569 / $16.95	
VOL. 3 – HARD ROCK	00699573 / $16.95	
VOL. 4 – POP/ROCK	00699571 / $16.99	
VOL. 5 – MODERN ROCK	00699574 / $16.99	
VOL. 6 – '90S ROCK	00699572 / $16.99	
VOL. 7 – BLUES	00699575 / $16.95	
VOL. 8 – ROCK	00699585 / $14.99	
VOL. 9 – PUNK ROCK	00699576 / $14.95	
VOL. 10 – ACOUSTIC	00699586 / $16.95	
VOL. 11 – EARLY ROCK	00699579 / $14.95	
VOL. 12 – POP/ROCK	00699587 / $14.95	
VOL. 13 – FOLK ROCK	00699581 / $15.99	
VOL. 14 – BLUES ROCK	00699582 / $16.95	
VOL. 15 – R&B	00699583 / $14.95	
VOL. 16 – JAZZ	00699584 / $15.95	
VOL. 17 – COUNTRY	00699588 / $15.95	
VOL. 18 – ACOUSTIC ROCK	00699577 / $15.95	
VOL. 19 – SOUL	00699578 / $14.99	
VOL. 20 – ROCKABILLY	00699580 / $14.95	
VOL. 21 – YULETIDE	00699602 / $14.95	
VOL. 22 – CHRISTMAS	00699600 / $15.95	
VOL. 23 – SURF	00699635 / $14.95	
VOL. 24 – ERIC CLAPTON	00699649 / $17.99	
VOL. 25 – LENNON & MCCARTNEY	00699642 / $16.99	
VOL. 26 – ELVIS PRESLEY	00699643 / $14.95	
VOL. 27 – DAVID LEE ROTH	00699645 / $16.95	
VOL. 28 – GREG KOCH	00699646 / $14.95	
VOL. 29 – BOB SEGER	00699647 / $15.99	
VOL. 30 – KISS	00699644 / $16.99	
VOL. 31 – CHRISTMAS HITS	00699652 / $14.95	
VOL. 32 – THE OFFSPRING	00699653 / $14.95	
VOL. 33 – ACOUSTIC CLASSICS	00699656 / $16.95	
VOL. 34 – CLASSIC ROCK	00699658 / $16.95	
VOL. 35 – HAIR METAL	00699660 / $16.95	
VOL. 36 – SOUTHERN ROCK	00699661 / $16.95	
VOL. 37 – ACOUSTIC UNPLUGGED	00699662 / $16.99	
VOL. 38 – BLUES	00699663 / $16.95	
VOL. 39 – '80S METAL	00699664 / $16.99	
VOL. 40 – INCUBUS	00699668 / $17.95	
VOL. 41 – ERIC CLAPTON	00699669 / $16.95	
VOL. 42 – 2000S ROCK	00699670 / $16.99	
VOL. 43 – LYNYRD SKYNYRD	00699681 / $17.95	
VOL. 44 – JAZZ	00699689 / $14.99	
VOL. 45 – TV THEMES	00699718 / $14.95	
VOL. 46 – MAINSTREAM ROCK	00699722 / $16.95	
VOL. 47 – HENDRIX SMASH HITS	00699723 / $19.95	
VOL. 48 – AEROSMITH CLASSICS	00699724 / $17.99	
VOL. 49 – STEVIE RAY VAUGHAN	00699725 / $17.99	
VOL. 51 – ALTERNATIVE '90S	00699727 / $14.99	
VOL. 52 – FUNK	00699728 / $14.95	
VOL. 53 – DISCO	00699729 / $14.99	
VOL. 54 – HEAVY METAL	00699730 / $14.95	
VOL. 55 – POP METAL	00699731 / $14.95	
VOL. 56 – FOO FIGHTERS	00699749 / $15.99	
VOL. 57 – SYSTEM OF A DOWN	00699751 / $14.95	
VOL. 58 – BLINK-182	00699772 / $14.95	
VOL. 59 – CHET ATKINS	00702347 / $16.99	
VOL. 60 – 3 DOORS DOWN	00699774 / $14.95	
VOL. 61 – SLIPKNOT	00699775 / $16.99	
VOL. 62 – CHRISTMAS CAROLS	00699798 / $12.95	
VOL. 63 – CREEDENCE CLEARWATER REVIVAL	00699802 / $16.99	
VOL. 64 – THE ULTIMATE OZZY OSBOURNE	00699803 / $16.99	
VOL. 66 – THE ROLLING STONES	00699807 / $16.95	
VOL. 67 – BLACK SABBATH	00699808 / $16.99	
VOL. 68 – PINK FLOYD – DARK SIDE OF THE MOON	00699809 / $16.99	
VOL. 69 – ACOUSTIC FAVORITES	00699810 / $14.95	
VOL. 70 – OZZY OSBOURNE	00699805 / $16.99	
VOL. 71 – CHRISTIAN ROCK	00699824 / $14.95	
VOL. 73 – BLUESY ROCK	00699829 / $16.99	
VOL. 75 – TOM PETTY	00699882 / $16.99	
VOL. 76 – COUNTRY HITS	00699884 / $14.95	
VOL. 77 – BLUEGRASS	00699910 / $14.99	
VOL. 78 – NIRVANA	00700132 / $16.99	
VOL. 79 – NEIL YOUNG	00700133 / $24.99	
VOL. 80 – ACOUSTIC ANTHOLOGY	00700175 / $19.95	
VOL. 81 – ROCK ANTHOLOGY	00700176 / $22.99	
VOL. 82 – EASY SONGS	00700177 / $12.99	
VOL. 83 – THREE CHORD SONGS	00700178 / $16.99	
VOL. 84 – STEELY DAN	00700200 / $16.99	
VOL. 85 – THE POLICE	00700269 /$16.99	
VOL. 86 – BOSTON	00700465 / $16.99	
VOL. 87 – ACOUSTIC WOMEN	00700763 / $14.99	
VOL. 88 – GRUNGE	00700467 / $16.99	
VOL. 89 – REGGAE	00700468 / $15.99	
VOL. 90 – CLASSICAL POP	00700469 / $14.99	
VOL. 91 – BLUES INSTRUMENTALS	00700505 / $14.99	
VOL. 92 – EARLY ROCK INSTRUMENTALS	00700506 / $14.99	
VOL. 93 – ROCK INSTRUMENTALS	00700507 / $16.99	
VOL. 95 – BLUES CLASSICS	00700509 / $14.99	
VOL. 96 – THIRD DAY	00700560 / $14.95	
VOL. 97 – ROCK BAND	00700703 / $14.99	
VOL. 99 – ZZ TOP	00700762 / $16.99	
VOL. 100 – B.B. KING	00700466 / $16.99	
VOL. 101 – SONGS FOR BEGINNERS	00701917 / $14.99	
VOL. 102 – CLASSIC PUNK	00700769 / $14.99	
VOL. 103 – SWITCHFOOT	00700773 / $16.99	
VOL. 104 – DUANE ALLMAN	00700846 / $16.99	
VOL. 106 – WEEZER	00700958 / $14.99	
VOL. 107 – CREAM	00701069 / $16.99	
VOL. 108 – THE WHO	00701053 / $16.99	
VOL. 109 – STEVE MILLER	00701054 / $14.99	
VOL. 111 – JOHN MELLENCAMP	00701056 / $14.99	
VOL. 112 – QUEEN	00701052 / $16.99	
VOL. 113 – JIM CROCE	00701058 / $15.99	
VOL. 114 – BON JOVI	00701060 / $14.99	
VOL. 115 – JOHNNY CASH	00701070 / $16.99	
VOL. 116 – THE VENTURES	00701124 / $14.99	
VOL. 117 – BRAD PAISLEY	00701224/ $16.99	
VOL. 118 – ERIC JOHNSON	00701353 / $16.99	
VOL. 119 – AC/DC CLASSICS	00701356 / $17.99	
VOL. 120 – PROGRESSIVE ROCK	00701457 / $14.99	
VOL. 121 – U2	00701508 / $16.99	
VOL. 123 – LENNON & MCCARTNEY ACOUSTIC	00701614 / $16.99	
VOL. 124 – MODERN WORSHIP	00701629 / $14.99	
VOL. 125 – JEFF BECK	00701687 / $16.99	
VOL. 126 – BOB MARLEY	00701701 / $16.99	
VOL. 127 – 1970S ROCK	00701739 / $14.99	
VOL. 128 – 1960S ROCK	00701740 / $14.99	
VOL. 129 – MEGADETH	00701741 / $16.99	
VOL. 131 – 1990S ROCK	00701743 / $14.99	
VOL. 132 – COUNTRY ROCK	00701757 / $15.99	
VOL. 133 – TAYLOR SWIFT	00701894 / $16.99	
VOL. 134 – AVENGED SEVENFOLD	00701906 / $16.99	
VOL. 136 – GUITAR THEMES	00701922 / $14.99	
VOL. 137 – IRISH TUNES	00701966 / $15.99	
VOL. 138 – BLUEGRASS CLASSICS	00701967 / $14.99	
VOL. 139 – GARY MOORE	00702370 / $16.99	
VOL. 140 – MORE STEVIE RAY VAUGHAN	00702396 / $17.99	
VOL. 141 – ACOUSTIC HITS	00702401 / $16.99	
VOL. 142 – KINGS OF LEON	00702418 / $16.99	
VOL. 144 – DJANGO REINHARDT	00702531 / $16.99	
VOL. 145 – DEF LEPPARD	00702532 / $16.99	
VOL. 147 – SIMON & GARFUNKEL	14041591 / $16.99	
VOL. 148 – BOB DYLAN	14041592 / $16.99	
VOL. 149 – AC/DC HITS	14041593 / $17.99	
VOL. 150 – ZAKK WYLDE	02501717 / $16.99	
VOL. 153 – RED HOT CHILI PEPPERS	00702990 / $19.99	
VOL. 156 – SLAYER	00703770 / $17.99	
VOL. 157 – FLEETWOOD MAC	00101382 / $16.99	
VOL. 158 – ULTIMATE CHRISTMAS	00101889 / $14.99	
VOL. 160 – T-BONE WALKER	00102641 / $16.99	
VOL. 161 – THE EAGLES – ACOUSTIC	00102659 / $17.99	
VOL. 162 – THE EAGLES HITS	00102667 / $17.99	
VOL. 163 – PANTERA	00103036 / $16.99	
VOL. 166 – MODERN BLUES	00700764 / $16.99	
VOL. 168 – KISS	00113421 / $16.99	
VOL. 169 – TAYLOR SWIFT	00115982 / $16.99	
VOL. 170 – THREE DAYS GRACE	00117337 / $16.99	

Complete song lists available online.

Prices, contents, and availability subject to change without notice.

HAL•LEONARD® CORPORATION

7777 W. BLUEMOUND RD. P.O. BOX 13819 MILWAUKEE, WI 53213

www.halleonard.com